3 Women

3 Women

Stephen Bett

EKSTASIS EDITIONS

Library and Archives Canada Cataloguing in Publication

Bett, Stephen C.
    Three women / Stephen Bett.

Poems.
ISBN 1-894800-90-7
ISBN 978-1-894800-90-7

    I. Title.

PS8553.E834T47 2006   C811'.54   C2006-905459

Cover design: Bernard Gastel

Acknowledgements: Earlier versions of some of these poems have appeared in *Jacket, The New Quarterly, The Nashwaak Review* and *Quills*..The author wishes to thank Langara College for the time needed to complete this book.

Printed in Canada

Published in 2006 by:
Ekstasis Editions Canada Ltd.   Ekstasis Editions
Box 8474, Main Postal Outlet   Box 571
Victoria, B.C. V8W 3S1   Banff, Alberta T1L 1H5

Ekstasis Editions wishes to thank the following for their support of its publishing program: the Canada Council for the Arts, and the Province of British Columbia through the British Columbia Arts Council.

for Kelly, with love

CONTENTS

3 Women

Those Godawful Streets of Man (1st St.)

It's like he said, the
godawful streets of man
except in my head
               presently,
they run to closed-
off boxes

Godawfulness in each one
each one at full head,
               a stubbornness
of cul-de-sacs, culled
& stuck there

Sacks that weigh against
tomorrow, make night
a heaviness, the true
heft of godawful
despair

Those Godawful Streets of Man (2nd St.)

And of woman. Everything's fender
slashed, smashed, broken, relationships crack-
ing apart all over the road, love doesn't
last a green light without crisis, kids
filled with amber & entitlement.

Therapists pick up business, open more
shop. And their women/men head thru
windshields seething, air bags, brakes
failed, love blood spray-pooled
on the screen.

Their kids become
therapists.

Those Godawful Streets of Man (3rd St.)

It's the personal, not social,
that catches.
Streets of *insidious intent*, back-
alleys of *Do I dare?*
Sure people are dying by the thousands
hundreds of ways, irksome numbing
stats.

Millions dying inside, too, off-camera,
cross-wired circuitry only just now
taking on generic interchangeable
modular labels.

Those Godawful Streets of Man (4th St.)

The boxes in one's head
eerie de Chirico
expanses
Crossed shadow
rutted, burned thru
pathways

Tight grid link,
wiring frayed

Hurt of love affair
gone bad,
boxes in that
too

Rooms full of heartache
— no vacancy —
right up there
in the brain

Those Godawful Streets of Man (5th St.)

Keep moving,
re-stack the boxes
in your head

Like zeks in the
gulags, they say,
move a pile
one place
to another
& back again

The point being
— there isn't one

Those Godawful Streets of Man (6th St.)

The streets are still out there
full of the usual disasters,
psychic & otherwise
(pending, impending)

Icy, frozen   Unlike those
mental boxes, fluid row houses,
neurotransmitters firing instant
distress messages

microscopic in space
unbearably vast
in time

Those Godawful Streets of Man (7th St.)

Each part of a recent
life, interlinked forms
Absorb each other, bleed
into each other

How to get out of
them, any one of them?
How limp, crawl,
squeeze

out of one's own
broken, self-
absorbed
head?

Those Godawful Streets of Man (8th St.)

Crate up the whole thing
throw it down the stairs
throw it into the street

All the boxes in one
mound, all heads
turned, looking,
what's inside

Just a head of pain un-
coiled, shredded wire
sticking up in spikes
across the roadbed

Those Godawful Streets of Man (9th St.)

Back in the street then
the breakage, breakage
what are our lives for
what singularity
breaks head & heart

Too many, too much
it all goes in, goes
out, drips from curb
down the drain

Whose life is this,
whose that, who doesn't
choke when the
love runs down

Those Godawful Streets of Man (10th St.)

Distress message received,
absorbed, there *is* no point
but feeling puts there

What felt such joy
rides out despair
runs down, so
godawful

like the sped-up high
when it comes
crashing down

Those Godawful Streets of Man (11th St.)

Bring it all back
in line, eerie rows
boxes lock to light,
fire shots into vast darkness
shell casings down the stairs
down drains

Bring it all back
catch shadow on
bled form, on grid,
on spiked &
shredded wire

Those Godawful Streets of Man (12th St.)

They're building on the godawful
streets of man, they're building
households of pain

They're building people too,
to fill them

Nerves frayed like over-spliced
wire & inaudible hearts
shorn

They're building handsome houses
with people inside
torn to shreds

For the Nine Guys

My literary buddies
at our monthly dinner
& wine piss-up
gossip, laugh & moan
about our lives

Best joke: Canadian version
of *The Scarlet Letter*?
Fuckin' Eh

The sweet young things,
the ex's, & kids
who've disowned us
one by one

Seconds, for the Nine Guys

Tonite, for some odd reason, staring into
the meat stew one of us brought
we get onto the subject of
psychopathic serial killers
the three or four big names from
around the world & the two
in our own back yard
Wackos who get something
(god knows what) off on
killing people in perverse & dis-
gusting ways & chopping
up the remains

Next, a lengthy debate between me &
Mark, drunk, gassed (holds cushion
to his chest when looped
—sheer giveaway)
About the value of traditional "liberal arts"
education, one defending, one arguing
who really gives a rat's ass anymore,
don't make first year English
compulsory & then just the
three nerds, geeks, dorks
in school will actually
want to take English
& the rest of us can
all take off home,
eh

Minimalist Pieces Following Dissolution of a Three Decade Marriage

The Grammar of Separation

Pronouns will now be easier
for you, "we" was always "I"
(in company, esp. her family)
               & antecedents
were already completely out
of reach

*

Scales of 1 - 10

First day after separation
go lock on to a giant Tylenol: 2 (maybe a 3)

Drive it off the lot as a silver German sportscar: 6

*

The "ex-" back-seat driving thru bends on life's
many little journeys (in our case emphasis "little"): 1

The Audi TT Coupe holding the road w/out shrewing or screeching: 8

*

Back-seat driver? Consumer reports on back "half" seat
recommend visiting a guillotinist before use

*

The little brochure TT cut-out makes a perfect fit taped over
the appropriate head & shoulders on the old family photo
Even the kids look excited about it ten years down the road,
and yours truly's smirking just thinking ahead

*

Both leather seats warm up, touch of a button
Little known German affection toasts infamous British reserve

Too late for you though Poor circulation Hands, feet, mood
Foot in mouth Mouth in gear Gloom pumped out like
toxic bilge Score that as engulfed, engulfing

*

What was the point? What was the fucking
goddamn point? Really, I'm serious
Living together like Cocteau's *Enfants Terribles*?
Like conniving, then imploding siblings?

More like slow rolling resentment You kept
secret notes Toted up kitchen chores, &c.,
clicked "record" on hidden tape so you could
"compare" levels of verbal abuse All this
your nervy, preferred octane

How do you spell entrapment?

p-a-t-h-e-t-i-c (more than *pathos*)

*

Talking to my friend Mark for hours on the phone
is a gallows-humour kind of mood-altering
experience Maybe one of the big pharma-
ceuticals should clone him, shrink him
to pill size, go "public" with the latest
in SSRI's— *Marzac*

*

with thanks to Trevor's keen eye

I have absolutely no respect for any
poet who whines about his ex-wife
having it off with some other guy
Besides, mine is half Scots And Scotland,
another (English) friend reminds me,
is sparsely populated for a reason
                              Auch laddie,
nae a kind word touch hug kiss
in over two decades Even more,
& in fact, precisely none

*

Coldheart. Stoneheart. "I don't *do*
warmth & affection."
Except for the kids of course & the
family dog, "sweetie," "sweetheart"

*

27

More Sad Advice (after Creeley)

"Hi, how's it going, how're you doing?
How's the condo search"?
Gimme a break! You chew down the
prime years of my life, I was even (like you)
strictly monogamous (such a putz)
I don't talk to you, comprendez?
Stay out of what's left of my life
Don't make a meal of it Dinner's over,
put away your fork

*

Wire-taut tendons, fight or flight mind,
cup half empty (even sleep one eye at the ready)
And too lethargic to go for help
Like "lighten up" —your own brother's lifelong advice
Massage Yoga Chemicals Whatever...

*

Too *busy* running around in circles to *make*
a "life" Saturday nights July—
making up endless banks of "quizzes" (absol. unreal)
for next year's classes to memorize/forget/whine
abt/resent you for (Hello? Duh!)
Who's on first? Who's at bat? They can't *give* tickets
away to this one— the single-A anal league

*

Riding the slow crest of waking up this morning
I wanted hopelessly, even so, for you to hug me hold
me without being asked, then surface thinking for years
touching you at all was like squeezing back black ice anyway

*

The old Scots' joke— hanging out toilet paper to dry.
No mortgage, no debts. House worth nearly a million.
Mutual funds, equity funds, locked in RRSPs. Another six
figures. Household income nearly triple the national average.
Top five to ten percent (Stats Can). No actual holiday trips —ever.
Furniture hand-me-downs. So what the pensions are minimal,
even "crap"? "Don't ever even *think* about the "R" word
before you drop, asshole!" &c. And what's left over goes to the
kids (despite two faculty parents & the kickstart of
major scholarships).
Mom so anal they won't want that wind-dried paper.
Buy it straight off the billboards, soft triple-ply
ready to roll. Like a red carpet. Into a future already
sectioned, lined out.

*

Good times? Memories? (See above)
The pleasure now is in spending that
filthy lucre.

*

Divisions of Labour

cooking vs cleaning up
floors vs toilets, tubs, & sinks
laundry vs ironing, vacuuming
so far, fair enough

plumbing —nope
electrical —yeah right
handyman —'scuse me?
scullery boy
bell hop
bus boy
go-fer
(on call, all purpose)

I'm thinking thumb
the yellow pages
cut the cheques

*

Reality News

Now she discusses separation terms,
financial issues, child support, house
maintenance like some vague, former
business acquaintance   Either that or spews
hysterical Nickel & diming And then hangs up

What's wrong with this picture?

What's *still* wrong with
this picture?

*

After Two Months Separation

Every night I dream backwards
overwrought, anxious we are
breaking apart barely before
starting out, breaking apart
before our kids come into view

Jumpstarting custody issues over
teenagers   Born right into the
pain-loaded face of adulthood

*

Get beyond it, even though you (I)
never will Get beyond it a.s.a.p. just do it, even impossible
Boomers   Stats   Clichés   Hitting the wave, late as usual

*

And while you're at it give me back
the prime cuts of my life
The ones you locked in the freezer
God let me thaw before I die

And give me back my children,
the two you slow-poisoned w/ a lifelong
litany of disrespect   Weekly diet of
questionable sleights, put downs
Kangaroo court now closed

The kids'll figure it out by age 25 max,
pop popped out by the big "D," the incessant dis'

'Teach' them I'm the one who's *got a problem,*
self-centred, irresponsible (good parenting)
your own nature bunkered down in the humour-
less dark   So deep a battery of psychs couldn't
penetrate with the latest in cluster bombs
aka "daisy chain" cutter
Not that you'd bother to call in a second round of
hits from your extended-medical-covered therapist

Daisies pull their own chains
we're told, eventually
flush pieces of themselves
perhaps you'd go that route too
end up neighbours in
psych city

*

Single Advice?

Don't marry when babies
Don't grow up together
Don't follow the same career path
Don't wait 13 years to have kids
(don't need the PhD first to be Super-Mom)
Don't "cocoon," don't become
one person one body 1.5 minds
Don't let lethargy & cowardice
gang up & lock the door

*

A Grammar of Emptiness & Longing

Thirty years wishing you
were someone else

Three decades wishing I
was someone else.

Boxes of Faith

First family gathering since we
signed the separation papers
our son's 17th birthday

& my sister later said you were
weeping briefly in the kitchen
slight reflex gagging, I imagine,
about all those so-called
"good times"

while numb in the living room—
I'm always numb in living rooms
at family deaths, even half-
unexpected ones

I left right after dinner want-
ing escape back to my new
place continue unpacking
boxes of books, boxes that

take me solely to my own
singular life (whatever that can
possibly be after all these years)
which I can now practise like
religion, suddenly immersed,
whenever I want, you

were right about that, it was
centred on myself & you
never could make a show
of any real faith

Another Ride

Held on for not-so-dear
life threw up this latest rupture
when a roller coaster
                    flattens out
the real scary part
about to drift off, float out
beyond the track

Your eyes scream louder
than your mouth clenched,
turn inward, see a horrid
thing staring there

Long as you could possibly want,
even longer

Then they shake, feel
like bursting out blind
thru the temples

A Disappearance

There's a certain, inevitable charm
to being dis'd & dismissed, one
doesn't have to go thru the
motions, any motions,
just do what one wants
—not that that ever solved
anything (as though there
was something to *be*
solved

But there's one less protocol
to spill out worry from that's
got to be a plus
                    Turn off the
tap shut down the
dripping faucet

Stir & drain

A willful dis-
appearance

To My 17-Yr-Old Son Abt To Start His University Career

Yeah, it's all an adult conspiracy Homer
wasn't necessarily Homer & there needn't be
any competitors to the oldest (let alone Lattimore)
translations there just are &, okay, it's a narrative
poem cuz a pre-literate story couldn't just be down-
loaded & burnt onto disc to pass thru the generations,
it's w/ in an oral tradition, & sorry it's a biggy in the
western canon (boom boom) wch., no, doesn't include
India even though they don't look Asian, but west was
west, like they say, & later Christian, & Buddhism started
in India before moving to China (to uproot the Tao) &
then Japan, trust me on this one, but you're right it's all a
mystery, incl. Indo-European, really, but it's *not* an effin'
conspiracy designed to piss off the MP3 generation abt
whom the West doesn't actually give a shit except for
their disposable dollars wch come from saps like yr dad

For My Savvy Daughter

Proud, my smart & lovely
daughter, you earned & got
the big bucks for school.

But shouldn't your scholar-
ship, to be truly in keeping
with current issues of
entitlement,
cover the cost of your new
eye-brow ring & self-
designed ankle tattoo

— half Om, half ancient Celt,
& darkly inked like a bold
Franz Kline or a full scale
retro-sealed guaranteed
deal?

Daughter

My cousin's husband gave me
a warning chuckle when you
were born—   hardy-har, daughters
always break their father's heart

Now at 22, dancer, scholar, power-yoga
over-achiever, fully signed-up member
of the entitlement generation
you shun all things mine (excluding
the ideology you inherited & excepting
my passions for books & for
Miles & Keith Jarrett

My only precious one, first born,
thrill of my life (& love & ever
adoring blood letting heart)
I'll surely win you back once you've
finished your doctorate at your
London School of Economics,
I'll fund a night course in ballistics
so you can knock off all the
corporate heads you spend your
youthful energy railing about
I'll "lazarus" mah-mah-my generation's
SDS, I'll fund (from my RSPs)
new chapters of Weathermen &
Bader-Meinhoff under your leadership
since summer jobs with Greenpeace
have taught you the small "c" hypocrisies
of corporate puke-raking

And I'll remember my favourite
summer holiday with my adorable girl
—first up at 14 reading Naomi Klein's
No Logo, my gift you roared through
like a summer beach novel
Pulling into the only gas station
in town, a Shell, you howling &
screaming thru open windows
how dare I w/ Shell Oil up
to their eye-barrels in atrocities
against Kenyan martyrs
Then noticing the two 16-year-old
boys pumping gas, biting your tongue,
too late, they were so cute,
which was of course your
dad's fault too

Every one of those years
one to twenty-two
I'd take a bullet
in the head
for you
— even one by
mistake

The New 21st C Boomer Bummer

The post-divorce "ownership" of
two abodes, mortgages, taxes,
insurance (plural, plural)
two kids in university
tends to have one,
month end

riding a layer of sweat
over a line of bank credit

Three Observations at Mid-Morning for You

1.

All those dickhead editors & self-declared
geniuses pontificating for a moratorium on poetry
on the basis of its current overabundance (abt wch no
doubt they're right on one score, 98% being crappola)
—these self-purveying windbags of logic would close down
their own air shafts, along with the supposed "readership" to
which they incestuously trade & disseminate "opinions" about all
practises in the "poetic arts," living & dead

2.

Noteworthy (?) the way a very bourgie real estate agent
I spent a few sterling moments with responded to each
& every one of my tidy little quips with a fully
appropriated "right on!"

3.

My dear old prof, I've discovered on the web,
has become an Emeritus (click) *"without email"*
(end click)

Thick

You're "thick," she screamed
harshly

& it wasn't until later
taking to account her lovely
& engaging lithp

that I realized she was merely
questioning my sanity

Curtains

I'm too much inside your
head? Sitting here reading a
Danilo Kis novel? About the torture
of Bolshevik Jewry under Stalin?
In this odious little plastic fortified
chain hotel room?

Gimme a break. Spare me.
The last place I want to be right
now is behind the shifting iron curtains
of your hyper-imaginary histrionics
my lovely history woman.

Bad Karma, Good Karma

1.

Charm & shelter a battered woman,
marry her, cheat on her con-
sistently for ten years,
force her to have three abortions (you don't
find pregnant women or mothers
"appealing"), refuse to consider
a vasectomy
because you might, quote, want
to have a kid some day
with another woman,
write a book you call
Gender Wars

2.

Some day Karma's going to visit
you, Karma's going to have you
kneel on the street Chinese
style, put a gun to the
back of your neck &
pull the trigger

Vesuvius

Sometimes you just
gotta vent, hon

Blow Vesuvius
give him the whole
job

Hanging Out

Okay, okay, okay
when the therapist says
hang in there
you really
start to think

hang in there

NB Suite 72: Weep Blood, Orph Sucks It Up

Whoops, can you believe it
weeks later, out of the blue
the black the RED, Orph's just
woken up in *Purgatorio* again
his gut in flames

Eury's volunteered for the *Inferno*
trickster fates have her shape-shifting
code, flinging darts, twisting Orph
the whole 180
                         He swallows each dart
w/ empathy for his spooked & frightened
love, each degree w/ patience for his
terror-struck loving love

And guess what, there's another locker
under the grassy knoll in *Purgatorio*,
it hides a snake tail, stings our Pro-
methean Orph each hour of the day

Dear reader, weep blood for him
it's red, goes down a bitter wine

NB Suite 73: Beyond the Reach of the Drill

Orpheus feels the lash
on his stomach
The bite in his gut

They are directed by
Eurydice, tormented in Hades
unwitting, unaware
She would love him to death
her tricksters sting him
drill him on rock

Snake's tail burns
from the grassy knoll
from the locker underneath
—the "black box" within

The box holds Eurydice's
whole life of terror
                            Orpheus
would try to swallow each
drop that leaks out

And in this never-ending close
love & terror 'live' buried
deep beyond the reach
of the drill

NB Suite 74: Reading Lesson

Lyre lyre, Orph's on fire
can't read the truth
with his neck on the wire

Eury's off the hook, long
out of Hades   — not really
there after all
                        Busy lighting
the cracks down to Purgatorio

Orph is starting to figure
it out, starting to "get it"
— *figura,* the shape
of her words

Truth is, relentless
to a fault   Truth is,
he'd be all in her face

Stick him in his cell
a bit more, teach
him to read

NB Suite 75: Omens

Orpheus in his cell
Receiving omens, signs,
figures of speech in
tea leaves

Sometimes they sting
sometimes sweet

Why so much trouble,
hypersensitivity, high
anxiety   Is this love
or bad connection

What she doesn't say
he hears, what he hears
she doesn't say

They sit in their corners
bleeding out their
mouths, their
fears

NB Suite 76: Eurydice's Negative Capability

Maybe tomorrow maybe
never says Eurydice live
in uncertainty   —savour
mysteries doubts without
any irritable reaching...

A "satori" of *not pursuing*
any viewpoint (di Prima at
Naropa rimes young romantic
consumptive & the American
Zen of "WOW")
Or Duncan (qtd. in Davey)
me *Protestant cannot bear*
be haunted by relative

But Orpheus doesn't do
ambiguity well   Panics him
chest shivers night sweats
Gnaws at mind & gut the
absolutes of his terror

Measure each moment for what
you would make of it love
says Eurydice begin with
the absence you daily
open your eyes to

NB Suite 77: To Adore is Not to Idealize

Bounce bounce —I sit
in my cell, patient
Listen to your courage
crack the floorboards
all the way from hell

Your mind in turmoil
the last few days
High anxiety, all
a swirl you say

When you argue to adore
is to idealize
When I argue to worship
is to idealize
When I tell you I'm
here when you need
to lean on me

& I'm here
(invisible & quiet)
when you need to work
thru things alone
in your head

you answer Okay,
now I adore you.

NB Suite 78: For the Sacred, and the Divine

In Hades they eviscerate
your stomach   — nauseous glow
legs numb   each arm run
currents   like fever, like nerves
nailed on a screen

But within the filaments   un-
holy stigmata   eyes locked
you say, one light   — divine
beyond singular inheritance
beyond all return
on darkness

Meantime in my gray cell
I practise living an ease
unknown to me
                 — it's the only
sacred ember I can
hold up to you

NB Suite 79: Another Round with Rilke

It *isn't* enough no matter
what moody things he
does in his cell
— or she in hers

They can't be reclaimed
don't want such things
cause love or pain or
lose focus when one
looks at them

No staring into the light
then, simply
                    stand guard
over the solitude
of the other, or else
just let go

Sometimes, even like
one, two, three   —gone

NB Suite 80: Fading ?

Now you endlessly repeat like
stars over Hades you
"*vant* to be alone"
to be in your withdrawn
& swirling head

(As if I'm choking to get
inside like some dumb
puppy heading for an al-
ready spilled-over bowl)

Being around you these
days is like draining a
whole bottle of downers
in one clean swallow
The irony being you then
call *me* bummed out

What does the doc say?
How does one spell
"fading interest"
without the ink
near run dry
halfway thru

NB Suite 81: This Eurydice in Trouble

1) Lifetime of absol. trauma, horrid abuse

2) Walls upon walls, & still more walls

3) Terror, & distrust (enough to fill each eye)

4) Fragile core (no carefree abandon)

5) "Irritation" factor, "prickly" bits (no playful tease, self-deprec.)

All the pores of this Orph
she calls *love of her life*
cannot flow enough tears
to soothe her troubled
soul

So Orph is told
it's best to go

NB Suite 82: Eurydice Proposes Forms of Suicide

A not unexpected but
still stinging note
hand-delivered from his
Eurydice

— she proposes to kill
herself, to choke what
little life lies at peace
in her, she's made
up her mind

What kind of death
this speaks to Orph
blank white of bitter
relief, black space
for dearest hope

What else can he do
sing his most
troubled song
her most
troubled
soul

his own horrible pain

— song that chokes
its own heart-
break end

NB Suite 83: Of Bards & Suicides

Eurydice twice dead, not
propitious says blind bard
of the round heads

And what of the living
sings Orpheus
where do the sighted
gather

In their separate cells
each one who loved
each to his own dark

round place

Cry beyond words
the strange cruelty
of his love's
terrible
end

NB Suite 84: Confused Advice

Weeks & weeks later Orpheus
sings caught in himself still,
his numb silence

A longing that doesn't
move easily away
                    — a could of / should of
sings behind him, plays
havoc with his mind

Makes him anguish today
dread tomorrow

One takes advice, piece
by piece, all sides, friend
by friend

It is easy to say she
had it all coming,
Orph alone tears himself
apart about where
it all went

NB Suite 85: Other Women

Orpheus sees other women
they are not Eurydice

I see other women
they can be warm,
they can be lovely
but they are not you

Eurydice died less gracefully
than she could wish to live
though with the same
high anxiety

& fallout dropping alive
fine poisonous glaze
on all the women
in Orph's world

NB Suite 86: Love Lies Down Like Infamy

Orpheus feels like drowning
Orbison song *It's Over* rings
his ears, her voice
squeezed out raw

So many women swamped by one
self-destructed voice, torments him
past now without past, present
without future

Eurydice's flood swept words of love
rot in his guts, like sea water
like infamy

Other arms, mere training buoys
don't begin to hold him

NB Suite 87: All Songs are One Song

That's all he sings now
Orpheus in the city
R & B on his lips
bouncing off concrete

You gotta tell me you're
comin' back to me

Baby, please don't go
Down to New Orleans
You know I love you so
Baby, please don't go

But she's long gone to Hades
& his lyre makes nothing sway

Trees stiff in small pads
between slabs of
sidewalk brick

NB Suite 88: No More Downloads, No More Burns

What's the point thinks Orpheus
no songs left,
shut down

Like Eury's life, like
twisted things
Songs for the living
or dead
never the twice dead
thrice dead, woman
who ghosted thru life
drew agony into herself

Orph's heart draining
fluid, valve burned out
It's over, it closes
It closes

Teacher

Our affair has ended
badly, accusations all over
the park   Despite protes-
tations about the one big
love in our lives

You tell me you are hurt,
angry, crying-sad & what else
in a blur I don't remember
Ditto & lost several pounds—
"issues" or mere "baggage"?

My bitterness reminds me
you did always opt for the
cliché when the psycho-
jargon wasn't at hand

Tell me about your hurt
tell me what hurt is you
were its teacher

Teacher II

Tell me about pain, it's
been with you all your
wretched, horrid life

Tell me how to grasp it,
live with it, wrestle it to
ground now you've

brought it headlong into
my life I don't know
what to do with it, how

leave it alone

Teacher III

It *is* your soul, your inner
grace I fell in love with, no-
thing else matters, ultimately,
or compares

Quitting now makes it all so
hopeless, so pointless, so
full of despair

They tell me, teacher, in your
grief you are merely be-
wildered   —other women

simple distraction, the
purest of logics for
managing pain

Teacher IV

Not provisional, you said
then reversed to free agents

Not marketable, I said
these our barbed codes

Hurtful, you grieve, so
like so, lessons in brink-

manship we flounder at
eyes open or closed

Teacher V

Teach me about grieving it's
not in the lesson plan, where
it comes from where it goes

Teach me why someone would
choose to live within it, what
pleasure derives what benefit

Teach me about grief, how unlock
its unfathomable logic, why its
course is pedantically required

Teach me how to draw it, paint
it, write its shape— I know none
of these things only scream

through the vast width &
length of its pain

Teacher VI

You blast me by email & a sub-
text of cracks comes bursting thru

Difficult, troubled, bossy
Intolerant, defensive, prickly
(guarded, walled in)
Blind, selfish, self-destructive path
Hidden behind fictions, phantoms,
misperceived slights
Sleights of hand, manipulation
Lovely, lonely, damaged soul
All these fault-lines speak
Psych 101—   gross insecurity

What do you teach, truly,
you teach me to be your
unpaid, victim
analyst

Teacher VII

Hey teach, I was missing you
so goddam much last nite
I called (lucky you weren't
in)   Our current assignment
is to grieve our torn affair
separately

I write "grieve separately"
hundreds of times across the
blackboard behind my head
like a mantra suspended over
a chalk ledge, like lines of
hopeless zeros in a ledger,
like there's no accounting the
incessant ways I just can't

stop, I just can't stop
just can't stop
thinking about
you

Teacher VIII

Teach me why grief just hangs
there, proverbial cloud on head
Maybe if I understand its nature
its cause I can work it back-
ward, scoop it up, blow it
away

Better, teach me, you watered
to the core this porous ache
how grasp its root, pull
it out of my guts

No you didn't teach me
enough but these bitter things
I'm not yet full

Teacher IX

Whoa, a new teacher's stepped up smart
to the front of the room, my own
analyst just dropped in to remind me
why I feel "conflicted" by your lessons

I have every right, he tells me, to be
loved & appreciated for who & what I
am, steer away from the "other" who
wants to "fix" me in (nebulous, in-
articulate) pieces

Today's lessons are floating there inert,
ambiguous, on the overhead, that's your
"projected" me you've got up on the
screen

You told me the whole thing goes
either way, a matter of choice

OK, I choose me

Teacher X

Hey love, I've been teaching
myself, I've been doing
the research

Severely abused women (or men),
how they never really get
over it, how their lovers suffer
a parallel kind of cycle

Passionate words one moment, aban-
donment the next, walls up &
down, doors opened, closed,
invited in, ushered out

Then comes the venting con-
fusion, then comes the mouth-
ful of hurt, then comes the
biting pain that seems for-
ever insoluble

Teacher XI

More research unmasks the Four
Horsemen of the Apocalyptic
Relationship

The deadliest of all being
"contempt"   Your condescension, love,
your finger-wagging, at my noviciate
status in the relationship
paradigm of, at best, ersatz value

Research & common sense
(that oftentimes lame fifth horse)
come down on the side
of my hunch, honey-bunch

So climb down off that mare's
haunches & kick up dust w/ me,
flagellating ourselves in a
new egalitarian glory
Make *that* our story

Teacher XII

Teacher raised the bar
ridiculously high this time
& gave me six months, boy
did I surprise the crapola
out of her
    And within a
third of that time—

Insight: A+

Epiphany: A+

Practise: lookin' real effin' good

Teacher XIII

I thought to call your
inappropriate sense of timing
three weeks ago an *oversight.*

Then last week, same thing,
a trifling piece of careless
thoughtlessness

Now you've just breezily
aired it out again. Let's be
little Miss Manners this time
& call it *insensitivity*

in its purest, most
natural inbred
form.

Teacher XIV

Hey teach, just found out
(my analyst's given another
damn straight tutorial)
I bin takin' classes from a
woman with somethin' called
Borderline Personality
Disorder (BPD)

— boundary, head-space, sec-
urity, trust "issues" galore,
common mostly to lifelong
trauma/abuse victims

Just read the book on it
too, & testimonials of other
students from all over the
seven seas
                just like these
BPDers — all over the
"emotional" map
pullin' you in, pushin' you
out, fast as they can reel

These classmates keep
pluggin' away til their
common response snaps in,
they spell it "m-i-s-e-r-y"
& drop the course

Teacher XV

The triple sign on the door says,
Class gossip. Support group. Debriefing.
Just found out from a classmate
that another teacher had had
a turbulent affair with her. A year.
Wrote a book about it. Poetry.
The sap.

She was obsessed w/ him, minimum two
different photos of him in every goddamn
room in her house. Lavished him with
love, adoration, expensive gifts.

Soulmate she'd waited all her life for, etc.,
after maybe a dozen (who's counting?)
failed relationships. Wanted to "fix" his
flawed bits too. Hey— she was the
"relationship expert" (read all the self-help
books during those failed relationships,
15 years in therapy, etc.).

Kept getting spooked tho & pulled back
("classic" case: abused child, battered wife).
Holed up behind "walls," "boundaries,"
great gobs of "head space." Even so,
claimed she'd let him in closer than
anyone ever.

Guy— nice dude. Open-minded, self-
reflective (touchingly naive?), agreed
to months of therapeutic "tweaking,"
got himself right up to speed. Clears
the bar each time she raises it. She's
amazed, a "miracle," adores him
even more.

So now she too's inspired to go back to even
more intensive therapy, latest hi-tech stuff
(EMDR), gets totally unstrung, moody,
pricklier than ever, projecting like crazy.

Xmas nite, she announces "this relationship
is not working for ME." Yup, blindsides him.
Why? She's "irritated" he's invading her
"head space." Two chief examples:
he spoke five seconds while she's reading
in bed, asked for a section of the morning
paper while she's doing her crossword.

He's still apologizing for her to friends.
Still walking on eggshells. "Troubled,"
he says, "trauma/abuse victim," cut her
some slack. Needs her "head space" &
"boundaries." Survival skills.

Oh gimme a break, groans one of the older
students (beautiful, experienced woman).
That's so '70s, those stupid psycho-babble
euphemisms— she's a nutter, totally sick.
Self-indulgent navel gazing for people
with too much time on their hands.
Put her back on this side of the
classroom fer crissakes.

Victim's Victim

You question my word sweet love
no-one has doubted my solemn
oath before, it no
lightly given hon

You may after all be what
they tell me, damaged
woman, destroyed woman
woman in unredeemable
"trouble"

For sure you can't see past your
own hurt, I understand
this, it too has
become mine

Hand Prints

Goddamit some days I
hate it still, your dirty
hand prints all over
my soul

That's how you left
it, started out with
grasp & grope
ended up with
the big shove

Just like your whole
life did to you, you
never could come
clean

Forever is a Form of Killing

Now you are gone from
me forever, even though
you are sick & troubled
with your horrid abused
life, I want so naively
to have saved you,
I want to have gone
all the way down
trying

Sweating It

So annoying in the gym
top 40, really top 3

over & over & over
pretty, pretty & pretty

while I'm sweating it out
like an idiot

thinking I'll play
harder, longer

while I'm still sweating
you out of my system

not close, by a long shot,
to your song or mine

Volatile

So the journey's come almost
full year   — what to say?
More gradient learned on the downers
Unsettling   Soul-mate
Heartbreak   Therapy   New
beginnings?

The ex miserable, bitter
now virtually hostile   Kids on
& off, mostly off   Snide, hurt
Love came big, went bigger
Two emotionally screwed up people
loving, banging heads together
poet & artist, volatile
Volatile & volatile

Volatile *before* mixing

Two-Way Pictures

First day back in my office
for the new semester, pictures of her
all over the shop, I jokingly offer
them to a friend down the hall, cut rate,
frames still good

He suggests keep them for the memories,
an interlude of middle-age love,
I say screw that, all the good
they've already done me do I
want heartbreak every day at
work too? I'm thinking pictures

pictures aren't about memory they're
about faded colour & pale witness,
they draw bitter blood right out
thru the eye sockets in two
dimensions two ways

Two Women

Like bookends on the year
cold   — & warm to a point
With the warm on a definite
cooling trend

Like a fire extinguished
smoke vapours, bearers of bad news

Sassy bratty witty charming
they said, open considerate wonder-
ful sexy   They said, needy im-
pulsive self-centred emotionally
immature

Highly desirable, hard to live
with, requires loads more self-control

Shelf done
High-maintenance & out
the door   Twice
Therapist in tow

Two Women, One Imaginary Bullet

One woman solid
as a rock, cold like
a snake

One woman both
joy & misery
of my life

This imaginary bullet
can carry only
my name

For All the Peggy Sues

Yeah, okay, maybe she
was a rebound
afterall

I dropped over 30 storeys
though, one per year,
bounced off my head

You, or you, or you
(hey hey Peggy Sue)
say it could be a world
of possibility

But I say I got me a
headache running
ground up

Valentine's

Hey new woman so
what was that "click,"
like they say,
you *did* get my
attention

Next step, this ah so
fresh bruised heart
or over to you & your
tango treated shoes
cha cha

Tell you what,
you just might click
that one too
flower in your teeth

The Red Dick Affair

First time I saw you I
wanted to kiss your mouth,
then each pink lip separately

It was that time of the month,
spent two nights together
you bemusedly called it
the red dick affair, does
that bother me?

To which I say au contraire
au naturel, no purple
prose at all

Blind Shots

You got any unlaundered clothes
in your wardrobe,
the new woman I've
been 'seeing' says you're
coming on to me like
a dirty shirt

says she can tell by the
look in your eye
says my eye looks like
taking up residence
in your house

I'd say she's pushing near-sighted,
you say she's pushing downright
blind

Two Minds

Two minds that don't
think alike

My license plate reads
BJS, which I like
to think of as
Bach, Johann Sebastian

On our third or fourth date
you laugh, B J Stephen

Sensitive type,
ruins everything for me

Believe That Too

So whaddaya say
another artist woman,
well what *does* one
say, been here before
(with disastrous results)

been there, been there
but each time's
different, so they
say, wanted to

believe that too,
wanted to seal it
somehow, with a
kiss— matte acrylic
or painter's glue

For My Mother

I bend to hug my
89 year-old mother
frail now & shrunken
I whisper thanks for
the gift she gave me
for all my life
an inner strength &
self-belief,
all that's got me
thru this last
two years

She adds your Dad
was pretty good too
& yeah I know that
also, he gave me love
without condition
without the stain
of judgement

Airs for My Heirs

A few fave pieces to play at (or on) my passing:

Bob Dylan, "Knockin' on Heaven's Door"

Procol Harem, "A Whiter Shade of Pale"

Glenn Gould, Bach's "Concerto for Piano & Orchestra, No. 5" (3rd movement)

Miles Davis, "He Loved Him Madly" (*Panthalassa* version)

Keith Jarrett, "Vienna Concert" (the whole gorgeous fucking thing)

The Kelly Poems: Kiki the Cat

Next time I come for a
sleepover (they're lovely, I'm
not complaining)
I'm gonna bring a big
tranquillizer gun for Kiki
jumping on my back &
head all nite, no?

OK a short dart, or better
yet (user/use-e friendly)
wear a crown of sublingual
Ativan pills in my hair

The Kelly Poems: Crushed

That crush thing you were
talking about, is it viral

d'you think cuz I'm
maybe catching it too

Say you love it when
I'm on top of you, inside

you, so nakedly unabashed
to declare for once it's all

like they say "easy peasy"
where I'd want myself

heart & soul to be
where I'd want to give

such ease, & thus receive

The Kelly Poems: Curled Lip at the Blues Bar

Blues club, last night,
totally jammed (in every
which way) one stool left
at the bar for us to share

Loner guy a few seats
down catches my attention
twitching his thin lips incess-
antly, wistfully stirring his
drink, hyper eyes darting
every so often between stage
& his wristwatch
Like a sorry puppy— I could
even think to take home
Like tourette's you correct me
or maybe psycho serial killer
(the neighbourhood's renowned
for disappearing prostitutes)

On a dare from me you sidle
down the bar, squeeze in beside
his stool & strike up conversation
(he's very "tight" you tell me
doesn't give you anything)

I'm chuckling away watching
you chat him up, your sweet
moxie, tilting, tossing your
head, shrugging, smiling that
cute cynical curled lip smile
of yours, that full lip I keep
wanting to kiss

And at that precise moment your
true self (still plenty to discover)
wires itself like a sequence of
perfect digital stills right
into my head

Now twenty-four hours later
they're still running thru
my mind, & I know I'm
falling into a narrative
headed somewhere
likely for sure

The Kelly Poems: Dirty Dancing the Blues
(with thanks to Big Road Blues)

You're 26 k.
from my heart

Until we're dancing
again— you ask
the singer I know
in the blues band
to do an Otis Reading
song

After the set the bass
player tells you to fully
appreciate the blues
you have to have had
your heart ripped out
of your chest a few
times, still beating

Guess that's why we
can get down so well
& dirty dance
the blues

The Kelly Poems: Park the Goddamn Plane

Sitting forever it seems
by the runway, one crazed
woman flies out of my life
& you, is it soft land or
crash land into it,
or me make stupid jokes
to welcome you with
my recklessly open &
still tender heart

I must respect your
airspace, you are gliding
in slow (special & precious
already by my calculations)
& naturally cautious about
betrayal in the landing
gear

I crave you safely low
altitude, well grounded &
wise as my instruments
so far clearly read you

There have been enough
broken hearts at such
airports, I promise
I'll not just blithely
fly thru yours

You've admittedly no right
to believe this yet, but I'd
really rather, when hangar
time is ready, just park
the goddamn plane

And never see you fly
in danger, at any risk,
or solo again

The Kelly Poems: Let There Be No Betrayals

You know you get to my
heart real quick, real direct
(which is what I desire, instant
honesty)
when you suspend the usual
psycho-jargon terms & excuses
(of which your work makes
you more than familiar)
— horrid terms like trauma
victim & Borderline
Personality Disorder

You say you envy me my
rare experience, intense love
gained & lost, but add
she didn't just hurt me
(she admits that) she
ignorantly & persistently
"played" with my head
"betrayed" me (woman doesn't
have a clue there)
For that you say she's
not just a nutter but a
"fucking bitch" & I'm OK
to think that too

She's truly sick, you say, &
if instead of her low-maintenance
"self-absorbed" life she'd been
saddled with job, kids & the
whole bit she'd have crawled
under the influence of social
services, self-medication,
alcohol, or both
— lucky to find your own desk
with its face-saving forms
& procedures

Sweetest heart, I don't need your
tender social service myself,
I want to *give* such tenderness
back to you that's never seen
daylight before

The Kelly Poems: Thank You

Thank you everybody, &
fuck youse, there's enough pain
& emptiness in our lives we'll
just have to take ourselves off
to more congenial places

leave bitterness & petty wrongs
on the rocks, up the creek, on
the wagon headed further west,
on a tanker in a container built
air-tight for double occupancy

I say we cover our tracks
I'm thinking Cinque Terra
on the Gulf of Spezia
you say southern France

maybe we can split the
difference, blow a couple
tanks of high octane, breeze
down the Oregon coast
in a season of love

The Kelly Poems: Heart Conundrum

It's a conundrum alright,
a 17th century conceit
Heart a bag of sand
dressed in barbed wire,
the whole lulled thing you're
afraid I'll snap

Heart I nonetheless intend
gently to infiltrate, peel
metal with my ancient teeth,
catch every grain like a
bruised universe on my
parched yet patient tongue

The Kelly Poems: Play Ball, They Say

You worry & brood
feel the risk of trust heavy
like a weighted bat
What can I say or do
friend for me in lineup
or mugshot
kneel against each
grounder
It is so small, so shapeless
a wisdom to say

But here only caught myself
wishing to lob, couldn't
do better than fly
out gloriously
ignobly
Be smarter this time
watch for the one
perfect one?

So— next up we'll
never "get" this slow
stupid game
so— just work the foul balls
on that third strike
You'd have me sit
all bases together
wait to feel you stroke
home the wholeness
of a grand slam

The Kelly Poems: Sorted

My eyes, my eyes
can't you see the pain

your eyes also
a misery
of sorts

Then we're all sorted,
each to each,
when you cried
into my neck
& my heart
still shudders

The Kelly Poems: Number Eleven for K

Kelly, your heart
is wary, but it *is*
there

right where it's
supposed to be
behind each smile,
smirk, puzzled
charm

it speaks through
your lips, jaded or
good humoured

full & quite possibly
the loveliest
I could ever know

The Kelly Poems: Steps

You hurt me, I hurt
you back, I'm sorry what
else can I say it was a
stupid stupid thing to do

Now the inevitable dance around
the question of belief, of forgive-
ness, of putting aside

And if I do, will you? And
who will stay more
vulnerable? And this too
a stupid dance made from
clumsy human steps

Steps only the gods
who aren't lame can
really break

The Kelly Poems: The Branding

Okay, okay cliché time
you can only hurt
the ones you love

and when your love
gives you even just
the slightest scratch

it festers in your
heart, it festers
like a branded mark

of searing shame

The Kelly Poems: Immeasurable

Forgive me I forgot to
thank you for your lovely
sweet words
I just forgot, forgot
forgetful me, the hours
make discordant
steps

Likewise my love for you
immeasurable
some days, easy to
say, over the top
others not so

We find our ways
measure smooth
measure rough,
& day by day
we sometimes
do forget

The Kelly Poems: Baggage

You are the love
of my life
you say

I've heard this
one twice
before

& wait how hard
the baggage hits
the floor

The Kelly Poems: Best Thing

You say I am the best
thing that's ever happened
to you

which is lovely, of course,
except a "thing" that
happens (!)

Then we argue semantics
in circles, as usual,
& my head spins
— a thing that spins

a "happening" in front of us
as we watch
silent, bested

The Kelly Poems:
For You Love, in the Face of my Ignorance

How can I tell you how sorry
I am at all you have to deal with
right now, how can I tell you I've
been a hindrance, not a help

I've just come across a pile of
dog-eared notes of all the horrid
things you've recently struggled to
deal with, you didn't make them

How can I say it but yes,
this is now *your* day, *your*
turn all my talk of being
here for you empty words
empty ears

Let me learn to be in the *right*
place, finally, get out
of the road, let you thru
the only way you know

The Kelly Poems: Sentences

Waiting on your sentence
takes more time & torture
than it takes to build
a concrete courthouse.

I'd rather wait on *your*
sentence when it opens
like a flower with the
word sweetheart.

The Kelly Poems: This Time

Let you down, love, let
the stress unravel me to
the limit this time

Wind me in the thread
of your arms, love,
like a spool,
make me strong again
return into myself

I'll land on my feet
as always, love, but
touching you this time
to keep my
balance

The Kelly Poems: For a Noble Woman

I'm not easy, for sure,
but I've stood by you &
yours a year now

Late nights on emergency row
mid-nights talking the poor kid
thru panic attacks
Living alongside near daily
howls of peacelessness

Who isn't "high-maintenance"
when it comes right down
to it, why do we do it
but for love & devotion?

The fact you stand by me
makes a world for me &
all that's noble in it

The Kelly Poems: Wino

Try as they might,
& for crissakes they have
(plenty of them, blood suckers)
they can't flood me
away from you

Last chance saloon
I drink you like
water, you go down
like dry white wine